EARL OF BOSWORTH

BRITAIN'S HOLIDAY WATERWAYS—a pictorial tour

BRITAIN'S HOLIDAY WATERWAYS

ROY J. WESTLAKE *ARPS*

D. BRADFORD BARTON LIMITED

Frontispiece: A quick word and a wave as two boats pass at the entrance to a lock on the Stratford-upon-Avon Canal—a scene typical of the relaxed, friendly atmosphere to be found on most inland waterways.

ISBN 0 85153 234 9

printed in Great Britain by Chapel River Press (IPC Printers), Andover for the publishers

D. BRADFORD BARTON LTD · Trethellan House · Truro · Cornwall · England

introduction

There are more than 2,000 miles of navigable waterways in Britain, offering a vast choice of scenery, ranging from the rivers of the popular—but rather crowded—Norfolk Broads to the lonely grandeur of the Scottish lochs that form a part of the Caledonian Canal. The quiet beauty of the Welsh canals contrasts with the bustling activity along the lower Thames and in between these extremes there are many miles of wide and narrow canals, rivers and lakes, all with a character and atmosphere of their own.

For the family seeking a not-too-energetic holiday, the Broads offer luxurious hire cruisers, lock-free cruising, adequate amenities and plenty of riverside pubs. The shallow lakes and rivers are the home of many species of wildlife and scattered throughout the area are interesting old windmills, originally used to work water pumps for drainage of the low-lying land.

To cruise the River Thames is to travel through history. In 1215, King John met the Barons at Runnymede and Magna Carta was signed in a riverside meadow. Throughout the centuries kings and queens of England have plied their royal barges on the river as a convenient means of travel between palace and great houses, whilst their subjects have used the waterway for the more mundane purposes of trade and commerce, water supply and drainage. In addition, Windsor, Hampton Court and Oxford all lie close to the river and are easy to reach from convenient moorings.

There are 45 locks between Teddington (the tidal limit) and Lechlade, which marks the upper limit of navigation for most craft. However, all are manned and little effort is required beyond steering and mooring one's own craft. On many reaches there are first class hotels and restaurants with riverside moorings. Although the lower reaches tend to become crowded at the height of the season there are numerous delightful stretches up-river from Oxford where one may enjoy peace and quiet at any time of the year.

For the canal enthusiast the choice is vast. Some canals follow the contours of the countryside with never a lock to be seen for miles on end, whilst on others it is impossible to travel more than a hundred yards or so without climbing a flight of muscle-stretching locks. There is little doubt that locks and swing bridges add to the enjoyment of a trip—in moderation! They provide a chance to stop and chat to other crews, or to take photographs. To try to cover too many miles in a day is to lose the essential attraction of a waterways holiday—the casual, relaxing pace through peaceful countryside, far removed from the snarl and bustle of motor traffic on crowded roads.

This book is an unashamedly admiring look at the more beautiful of Britain's waterways. Of the many miles available for cruising it can cover only a representative fraction, but perhaps these photographs will bring pleasure to those who already know the attractions and also serve to whet the appetite of the first-time hirer. One thing is certain—that once a holiday has been spent 'messing about' in a boat, no other holiday will seem quite the same again.

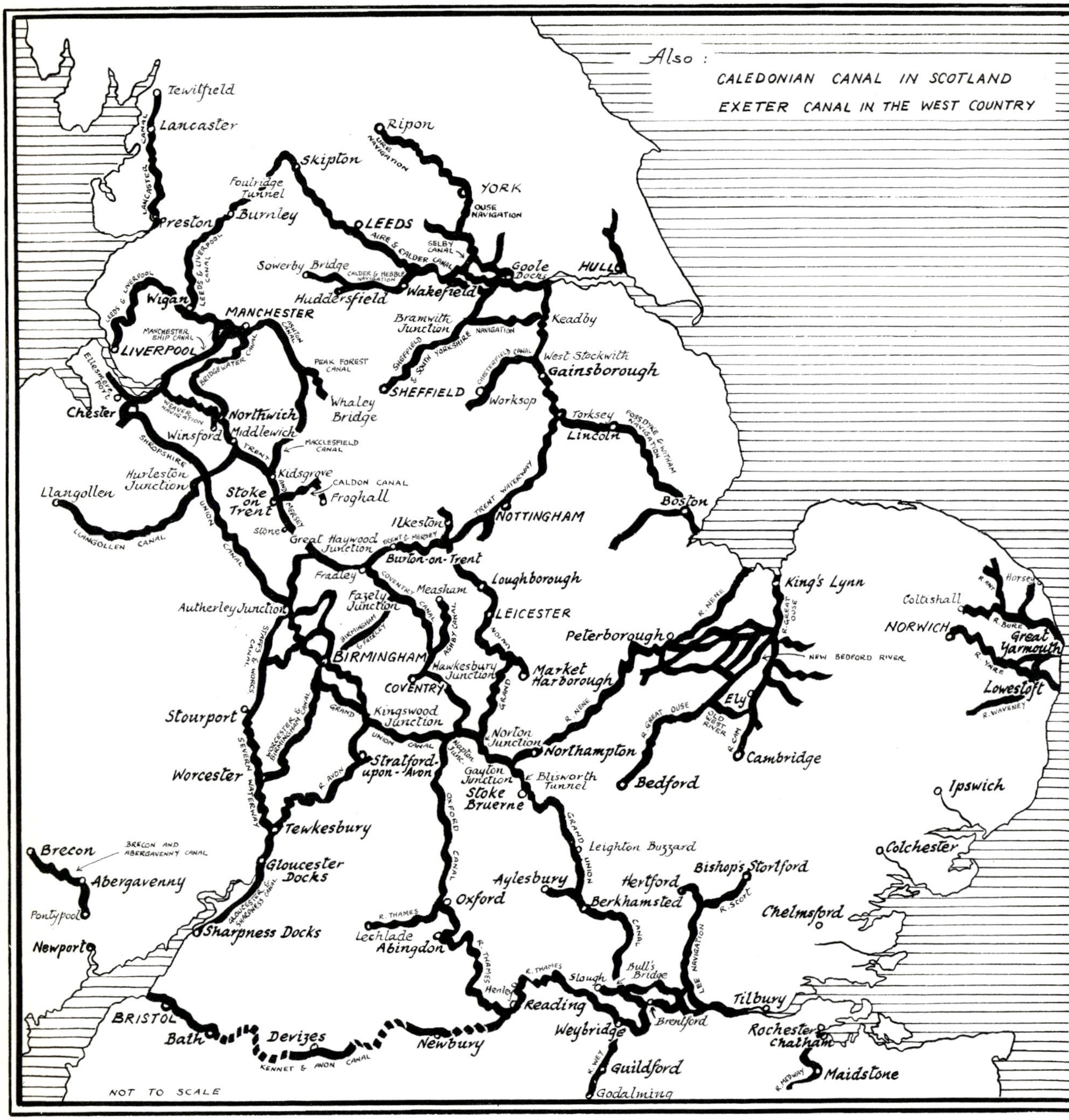

Also :
CALEDONIAN CANAL IN SCOTLAND
EXETER CANAL IN THE WEST COUNTRY
Tewitfield
Lancaster
LANCASTER CANAL
Preston
Foulridge Tunnel
Burnley
Skipton
Ripon
URE NAVIGATION
YORK
OUSE NAVIGATION
LEEDS
AIRE & CALDER CANAL
SELBY CANAL
Goole Docks
HULL
Sowerby Bridge
CALDER & HEBBLE NAVIGATION
Huddersfield
Wakefield
LEEDS & LIVERPOOL CANAL
LEEDS & LIVERPOOL
Wigan
MANCHESTER
MANCHESTER SHIP CANAL
LIVERPOOL
ASHTON CANAL
PEAK FOREST CANAL
BRIDGEWATER CANAL
Bramwith Junction
SHEFFIELD & SOUTH YORKSHIRE NAVIGATION
Keadby
West Stockwith
CHESTERFIELD CANAL
Gainsborough
SHEFFIELD
Worksop
Whaley Bridge
Ellesmere Port
Chester
WEAVER NAVIGATION
Northwich
Winsford
Middlewich
MACCLESFIELD CANAL
TRENT
Torksey
FOSSDYKE & WITHAM NAVIGATION
Lincoln
SHROPSHIRE
Hurleston Junction
Kidsgrove
CALDON CANAL
Froghall
Llangollen
LLANGOLLEN CANAL
UNION CANAL
Stoke on Trent
TRENT & MERSEY
Stone
TRENT WATERWAY
NOTTINGHAM
Boston
Ilkeston
Great Haywood Junction
TRENT & MERSEY
Burton-on-Trent
Fradley
COVENTRY CANAL
Measham
Loughborough
Fazeley Junction
BIRMINGHAM & FAZELEY
ASHBY CANAL
LEICESTER
Autherley Junction
STAFFS & WORCS CANAL
BIRMINGHAM
Hawkesbury Junction
COVENTRY
Market Harborough
GRAND UNION
Peterborough
R. NENE
King's Lynn
R. GREAT OUSE
NEW BEDFORD RIVER
Coltishall
R. ANT
Horsey
R. BURE
NORWICH
Great Yarmouth
R. YARE
Lowestoft
R. WAVENEY
Stourport
WORCESTER & BIRMINGHAM CANAL
GRAND
Kingswood Junction
UNION CANAL
Norton Junction
Northampton
R. NENE
R. GREAT OUSE
OLD WEST RIVER
Ely
R. CAM
Cambridge
Worcester
SEVERN WATERWAY
Stratford-upon-Avon
R. AVON
Norton Junc.
Gayton Junction
Blisworth Tunnel
Stoke Bruerne
Bedford
Ipswich
Tewkesbury
OXFORD CANAL
GRAND UNION CANAL
Leighton Buzzard
Brecon
BRECON AND ABERGAVENNY CANAL
Abergavenny
Gloucester Docks
Colchester
Bishop's Stortford
Hertford
Aylesbury
Pontypool
GLOUCESTER & SHARPNESS CANAL
Oxford
Berkhamsted
R. Stort
Chelmsford
LEE NAVIGATION
Sharpness Docks
R. THAMES
Lechlade
Abingdon
Newport
R. THAMES
Henley
Slough
Bull's Bridge
Tilbury
BRISTOL
Reading
Brentford
Bath
Devizes
Newbury
Weybridge
Rochester
Chatham
KENNET & AVON CANAL
R. WEY
Guildford
R. MEDWAY
Maidstone
Godalming
NOT TO SCALE

THE BROADS

The Norfolk Broads are undoubtedly Britain's most popular cruising area and have been for very many years. Miles of easy-to-navigate rivers and shallow lakes form an ideal area for leisurely and relaxing holidays. There are boats for hire in every conceivable shape and size, most nowadays complete with hot and cold water, refrigerators, showers, central heating, sun-decks, TV, etc.

Riverside pubs are sited at strategic points and the proprietors have years of experience in catering for the thirsty needs of waterborne holidaymakers. If it's entertainments you want, there are the bright lights of Great Yarmouth, and water sports—speedboat racing, regattas, etc.—on Oulton Broad.

The Broads are ideal for the novice. Commercial traffic is very light, there are no locks and few hazards to navigation. The worst fate that is likely to befall is to spend a few hours on the mud approaching Great Yarmouth as the tide retreats down river.

Although during July and August the popular rivers resemble the M1, it is still possible to get away from it all in the quieter Broads and on the upper reaches of the rivers. There are mile after mile of rivers, dykes and backwaters, plus of course the actual Broads, shallow lagoons formed from the pits left by peat-cutters. It is worth remembering that if you want to explore some of the remoter areas, you must choose a boat with superstructure that will go under the low bridges. The Broads abound in wild life. You will see water voles, probably otters and certainly the coypu. The latter—which looks like a large rat—was originally imported into East Anglia from South America for its fur. A few escaped and formed colonies amongst the reed beds. Wild fowl are to be seen everywhere—moorhens, the friendly coots, marsh harriers, bitterns and many others. The scene below is at Beccles, a popular mooring place on the River Waveney.

Tree-lined moorings by a grassy bank, in a backwater at Thorpe, near Norwich.

A never-to-be-forgotten sight is that of yachts tacking back and forth in the narrow rivers, their wind-laden sails adding colour and grace to the Broadland scene. Regrettably, cruisers are tending to oust sailing craft, but quite a few are still to be found making their leisurely way along the waterways.

Thurne Mill makes an attractive picture outlined against a typical Broadland sky. This is a restored wind-pump, originally used to drain the surrounding fields.

Waterside pubs are also a feature of the Broads—most provid excellent moorings, whether for a quick pint, or overnight stop This is 'The Ferry' at Horning.

A welcoming table an good moorings at 'The Rising Sun', at Coltishall. Perhaps it's a pity the glasses have already been emptied!

Dinghies on Oulton Water—a vast expanse ideal for all water sports. Regattas and speed boat racing are also held here.

Albion is one of the last survivors of the many trading wherries that plied the waterways of Norfolk and Suffolk. Now owned by the Norfolk Wherry Trust which was formed in 1949, she is a colourful sight with brightly painted cabin-top and hatches, and 40ft mast carrying one huge black sail. In their heyday, wherries carried mixed cargoes—coal, timber, bricks, grain, flour, etc.—to the village staithes. Twenty to forty tons were carried in one large hold and the boats were normally handled by a crew of two.

At one end of Horsey Mere is a staithe, or navigable dyke, leading to Horsey Mill. There are good moorings here and the mill, which is owned by the National Trust, is open to the public. Inside one may see the original mechanism and from the outside gallery on the top there is a magnificent view of the surrounding countryside.

Moorings at Horsey staithe, seen from the top of the mill.

A modern fibre-glass cruiser at Coltishall, on the River Bure. This type of boat is light and airy, easy to handle, and has nearly all the comforts of home. Coltishall is a popular mooring; there is a wide expanse of grass for children's games, and shops nearby.

This yacht makes ar attractive picture alongside one of th old mills on the Riv Ant.

Tree-lined South Walsham Broad, off the River Bure, has ample space fc mooring in pleasant surroundings.

Y715
QUEEN ANNE
W.K. BARNES (WROXHAM) LTD

cruiser mooring at
eedham, on the
iver Yare, no doubt to
l up with water from
e tap close-by. This
a busy place with
xtensive moorings,
el supplies, shops
nd restaurants.

peaceful scene on
e River Ant, near
udham.

Moorings at Ranworth Staithe, with Malthouse Broad in the background ... and popular area, at times crowded with boats jostling to moor. Ranw... often called the cathedral of the Broads and has one of the finest ... England.

THE FENS

After the crowded waters of the Broads, Fenland is a haven of peace and quiet. The area is generally considered to cover about 2,500 square miles, extending from south of Lincoln to Suffolk, and including parts of Norfolk, Cambridgeshire and Huntingdonshire. It was originally a low-lying swampy area, with silt beds and peat, thickly afforested in parts.

The Romans carried out some drainage work and efforts have been made continuously since the Middle Ages to reclaim the whole of the Fens. Drainage channels now criss-cross the area which has been turned into some of the richest farmland in the country.

Fenland has an undeserved reputation for being flat and uninteresting. True, many of the waterways are primarily drainage channels and must, of necessity, follow dead straight courses through level countryside. However, there are many stretches on the Rivers Cam and Great Ouse quite equal in beauty to the Thames. The small towns—St. Ives, Godmanchester, etc.—all have attractive backwaters and Ely, on the Great Ouse, is worth visiting for its cathedral alone.

The southern rivers are most popular for hire cruisers, mooring is no problem and there are plenty of shops, marinas, pubs, etc., to provide fuel for boat and crew.

These two photographs represent the extremes of Fenland. Left, a quiet backwater reflecting the many styles of architecture to be found at Godmanchester. Right, a long flat stretch of the River Cam, turned to silver by the setting sun.

The Great Ouse is noted for coarse fishing and other Fens rivers also offer good sport. Here a fisherman sits patiently as the sun rises on the Old West River. This once carried the waters of the Great Ouse before the cutting of the Old Bedford River and Hundred Foot drainage channels in the seventeenth century. Nowadays, it serves as a navigable channel between the Rivers Cam and Great Ouse.

Houghton water mill on the Great Ouse is a massive seventeenth century timber building in a peaceful setting. It is now owned and maintained by the National Trust and there are convenient moorings at Houghton Lock to visit this quiet backwater.

Overleaf: Hemingford Lock on the River Great Ouse, near St. Ives, comfortably takes two large cruisers with ample room to spare.

FARMERS GLORY

WISSEY
H.C. BANHAM
CAMBRIDGE

A closer view of the guillotine-type gate on Hemingford Lock. Few other British waterways employ this type of gate, but they are quite common on Fenland rivers. Although a little startling at first sight there are few problems in their operation. In theory, Hemingford is electrically operated and all one has to do is press a button. However, it often seems to be out of order—no doubt due to vandalism—and a great many turns of the low-geared handle are required to lift the heavy steel gate, although it is counterbalanced by another large steel slab behind the gate.

Another guillotine-type gate at Brownhill Staunch, again on the River Great Ouse. There is a lock-keeper here and the mechanism is electrically operated. A touch of a button makes light work of opening the gate and filling the lock. The looped chains on the side walls are useful for holding the boat in position, particularly when the lock is crowded.

Three large hire cruisers will just fit into Bottisham Lock, on the River Cam, not far from Cambridge.

'The Cutter' at Ely, is well known riverside pub with ample mooring space. This is also a good place t moor for the shops close-by, or to visit Ely's magnificent cathedral, the towers of which can be seen for many miles across the flat Fenland landscape.

By turning sharp left immediately above Godmanchester Lock one reaches a very pleasant backwater with moorings adjoining a park.

THE CUTTER

ROYAL OAK

BRIDGE
HOTEL
WHITBREAD

The fifteenth century bridge at St. Ives has a very unusual chapel built out over a central pier. The arches are quite low and slope steeply, requiring careful negotiation; multi-coloured streaks of paint on the masonry bear witness to many close shaves. St. Ives is a picturesque old town with several interesting houses of early date, as well as the remains of a priory. Oliver Cromwell lived near the town and his statue stands in the market place.

The Bridge Inn', at St. Neots, reflected in the waters of the Great)use River. There is a mainroad bridge a few yards upstream and, n the far side, a small concrete landing stage giving access to town nd shops.

RIVER THAMES

What can one add to what has already been written about the Thames? Whether viewed through the irreverent eyes of Jerome K. Jerome's 'Three Men in a Boat', who sculled lightheartedly from Kingston to Oxford, or from the viewpoint of an historian, it is one of the truly great rivers of Europe.

For holiday cruising, it is second only to the Broads in popularity and there are numerous firms along its length offering every manner of craft for hire. Below Teddington—the tidal limit—the river is controlled by the Port of London Authority, above this point by the Thames Conservancy. All locks are manned, many being electrically operated, and little effort is required from boats' crews.

Most towns on its banks take full advantage of their situation and provide good mooring facilities in pleasant surroundings. There is something very satisfying about mooring quietly and easily within a few hundred yards of a busy town centre, with no worries about yellow lines, time limits, traffic wardens, etc., or perhaps stepping ashore from a convenient mooring for a meal at a riverside restaurant.

A holiday cruiser about to pass under Windsor Bridge, with the castle in the background.

ne Thames at London, with the sun setting behind Big Ben and
estminster Bridge.

A pleasant place to go fishing on a lazy summer's day. No doubt in 1215 it bustled with activity, for it was here at Runnymede that Magna Carta was signed by King John and the Barons. A memorial close-by commemorates the occasion.

At Marlow there are good moorings alongside a park with this delightful suspensio bridge in the background.

On the Thames the approach to weirs is generally well protected by posts, etc. How ever, one should never ignore or take lightly DANGER signs. At Marlow the weir is i direct line with the approach to the lock and that deceptively smooth patch of wate by the sign is actually the extreme edge of the weir.

MOORING

DANGER

What better way to spend a hot summer afternoon. A peaceful pint, or perhaps a meal, moored alongside the 'Angel Hotel' at Henley.

Helmsman's-eye-view of the river above Oxford, with stratocumulus clouds scudding across a summery sky. Note the collapsible windscreen—even on the Thames it is useful at times to be able to reduce overall height when going under low bridges, etc.

Sonning is probably one of the most colourful and best kept locks on the river. Here four cruisers ease into position alongside banks of multi-coloured roses and neatly trimmed lawns

onning bridge not
r away marks one of
e oldest crossing
laces on the Thames.
here is a charming
llage just down the
oad with timber-
amed cottages and
n old mill.

The view from Pangbourne bridge.

A cruiser approaches Goring Lock in late evening, under the watchful eye of the lock-keeper. If arriving outside the normal hours of attendance (or during the mid-day lunch break) crews are allowed to operate the majority of Thames locks themselves, but only manually. This is rather a slow procedure on large locks as the wheel operating the sluices and gates is very low geared. Normally locks are attended until around sunset, but in the morning those wishing to be away at the crack of dawn will have to reconcile themselves to a certain amount of exercise. Often this is well worthwhile as the river can be very beautiful on a bright sunny morning with the mist still rising.

Pangbourne Meadow is a favourite mooring for many people. With reasonable depth of water close to the bank, one can step straight from the cockpit on to soft springy grass. A favourite place too for anglers, young and old.

There are also moorings below Wallingford Bridge, in delightful surroundings, with trees overhanging the far bank. Wildfowl—usually more tame than wild—are to be found everywhere on the Thames and here a group have gathered to be fed as soon as a boat moors.

Below Goring Lock the river runs through a narrow wooded gorge between the Chiltern Hills and the Berkshire Downs. There are good moorings here with a well used riverside path.

A dramatic view of the river through one of the arches of Wallingford Bridge.

Many reaches of the Thames are delightfully rural, although not far from large towns This view is near Long Wittenham in Berkshire. Below, a hire cruiser leavin Sandford Lock.

The same church spire can be seen on the skyline as cruisers prepare to leave Abingdon Lock.

Sir Gilbert Scott's fine six-arched bridge at Clifton Hampden marks the boundary between Oxfordshire and Berkshire.

solitary church spire and huddle of mellow buildings make a delightful background o the river at Abingdon, in Berkshire. There are many interesting old buildings ere, including some that date from the days of its prosperous abbey, dissolved nder Henry VIII.

Above Oxford the Thames becomes narrower and meanders through low-lying meadows. Here two boats—one from its base at Aynho on the Oxford Canal, the other from Southampton—share a quiet stretch of river at Eastertime.

Sunset at journey's end! Melodramatic, but literally true. Lechlade, in Gloucestershire, marks the upper limit of navigation for most cruisers. Small boats can penetrate further towards the source of the Thames—still many miles away, near Cirencester. A statue of Father Thames marks the exact spot where the river rises from a small spring.

THE CANALS

Towards the end of the eighteenth century, Britain's canal network represented the quickest, cheapest and most efficient means of transporting goods. Coal was carried from the major coalfields to centres of population and industry, sea-sand was transported from the coast as fertiliser for inland farms and a great number of other cargoes travelled along various sections of the system.

The man who began it all was the third Duke of Bridgwater, who in 1759 obtained powers to build a canal to carry coal from his mines at Worsley, to Manchester, eight miles away. The Bridgwater Canal was highly successful and this was the signal for a rush of canal building, producing navigations of all types, sizes and gauges.

With the coming of railways canal trade decreased, although some canals continued to compete successfully for a number of years. Generally, however, the expansion of the railway network marked the gradual decline of canals and eventually many became derelict.

Commercial use has continued to decrease until today it is rare indeed to find working boats anywhere on the system. To counter this, however, the increase in pleasure cruising over recent years has been phenomenal. What started as a spare time pursuit for a few dedicated enthusiasts has developed into a large scale holiday and leisure activity as more and more people discover the pleasure of travelling slowly amidst beautiful surroundings, well away from the congestion and noise of overcrowded main roads.

The future of existing canals now seems reasonably secure and other neglected and semi-derelict waterways are gradually being re-opened through the voluntary efforts of various canal societies and the dedicated work of the Inland Waterways Association. Were it not for them there would be few canals (or rivers) left upon which to cruise.

The Llangollen Canal is one of the most attractive and popular in Britain. It was built in sections and completed in about 1808 when a navigable feeder was constructed to carry water from the River Dee at Llantisillo to the northern end of the famous Pontcysylite Aqueduct. Although narrow, this short section is particularly beautiful, winding through the mountains with different views at each bend until one reaches the wharf at Llangollen, high above the town.

Between Pontcysylite and the junction with the Shropshire Union Canal at Hurleston, there are a number of these sturdy white-painted draw-bridges which have to be lifted every time a boat passes. Most give access to farmers' fields, but occasionally one has to hold up traffic on minor roads. In theory, all are counter-balanced, so little effort is required. In practice, a weighty member of the crew on the end of the lifting beam is undoubtedly an advantage.

The lower three locks on the Llangollen Canal at Grindley Brook are of conventional type with a pound (short stretch of canal) between each. However, the top three form a staircase, that is, the bottom gate of one forms the top gate of the next in line. A different technique is required on these, particularly when travelling uphill and this sometimes causes confusion. A main road crosses the canal at this point and there are usually a few sightseers to witness any mistakes! More important, there are good moorings above the top lock, with a tap for filling water tanks, and shops nearby.

Overleaf: Still on the Llangollen Canal, Willeymoor Lock is in a completely rural setting. Here a narrow boat from the Anglo-Welsh hire fleet based at Trevor prepares to leave the lock.

In South Wales, the Brecon–Abergavenny Canal is a 'dead-end' waterway, with unfortunately no connection to the remainder of the canal system. It is 33 miles in length and has a number of interesting features, including the modern lift bridge at Talybont. This is easy to operate, but very low-geared and slow in use. The local wildlife soon gather when one moors and here a family of swans waits—none too patiently—to be fed.

All canals are shallow, but some are more shallow than others. Heavy commercial boats used to scour out the bottoms and kept canals free of weed, but nowadays with little commercial traffic many canals have become silted. The Brecon–Abergavenny is beautifully clean, but shallow, and the illustration above shows a familiar problem. A moderately deep draught boat attempts to moor some distance from the bank; easy enough if the plank is sufficiently long, but often it is advisable to seek a deeper mooring elsewhere.

OWAIN GLYNDWR

ovilon Wharf on the Brecon–Abergavenny Canal is a busy place at weekends, with oat club moorings, waterpoint, winding-hole (for turning larger boats) and vaterbus'.

In contrast, a boat leaving one of the wide locks on a lonely stretch of the Shropshire Union Canal.

The Oxford Canal between Braunston and Hawkesbury Junction is attractive and rural, although not far from several large towns. There are a number of wooded cuttings and also long, straight stretches where the old canal was shortened in 1829.

It is a great deal easier to park a boat than a car at Stratford-upon-Avon! This narrow boat is moored in the canal basin, alongside the lock leading into the river Avon. The Shakespeare Memorial Theatre is in the background and one can moor even closer to this by going through the lock and travelling a hundred yards or so downstream. An early morning picture this—usually the park is teeming with visitors of all nationalities.

A rather daunting prospect—this flight of narrow locks on the Stratford-upon-Avon Canal stretches as far as the eye can see. The canal was restored by voluntary labour between 1961 and 1964 after being derelict for many years and is now one of the two waterways in the country—the River Wey is the other—administered by the National Trust.

The canal entrance, under a neat footbridge in th basin at Kingswood Junction, where it connec with the Grand Union Canal.

A peaceful scene near Wilmcote, only a mile or so from the bustle of Stratford-upon-Avon.

The well known Edstone Aqueduct, on the Stratford-upon-Avon Canal, is basically an iron trough mounted on piers to carry the canal over a road and two railway lines. Aqueducts are not as frightening as they may seem—usually a boat will even steer itself across if left to gently bump along the narrow channel.

A very interesting feature of this canal is the black and white barrel-roofed lo cottages—unique on the canal system.

Another unusual feature is the construction of many of the bridges. These are of tw completely separate cast-iron sections, with a two inch gap in the centre, throug which the tow rope could be passed. This saved the cost of building a wider bridge take the towpath—usually at the entrance to a lock.

n the north of England, the Leeds and Liverpool Canal passes through superb scenery as it winds over the Pennines. A typical swing bridge, near Skipton, in Yorkshire.

A wide stretch of open canal, near Gargrave.

The Bingley Five Rise —five staircase locks —lifts the Leeds and Liverpool Canal 60ft in one huge step. This is one of the wonders of the waterways system and the massive gates and deep locks can present quite a daunting appearance. The flight is well maintained by British Waterways, but the horde of sightseers at weekends does nothing to help crews passing through.

Cruising on the southern section of the Oxford Canal in early spring. Easter is often a good time to hire a boat, but it is worth remembering that traditional style narrow boats offer very little weather protection for the helmsman. Therefore, warm waterproof clothes are essential for 'out-of-season' cruising. More conventional boats often have pram-type hoods and side screens enclosing the cockpit —these are more comfortable but an unmitigated nuisance on heavily locked canals, or those with numerous low bridges.

This boat is leaving Shipton Weir lock. At this point the canal joins the River Cherwell (or vice versa) and they share a common course until the next lock.

The Oxford Canal, planned by James Brindley, was one of the earliest to be built and was completed in 1790. It is a contour canal, that is, it follows the contours of the land instead of relying on extensive cuttings and embankments. The village at Cropedy Lock is one of the most attractive on this canal. Peaceful now, it was the site of a battle in 1644 between Roundheads and Cavaliers during the Civil War.

Overleaf: Typical of the tranquillity of the canals is this scene on the Trent and Mersey Canal.

Either an original narrow boat, or purpose-built replica, and obviously kept in first class order, this craft makes a pleasant picture moored on the Trent and Mersey Canal near Haywood Junction, where it is joined by the Stafford and Worcester Canal.

The casual approach to locking on a hot summer's day. This pleasant scene is also on the Trent and Mersey Canal, which is 93 miles long and includes rural and industrial sections. At Harecastle there is a tunnel $1\frac{3}{4}$ miles long and the canal also connects with the Anderton Lift, a remarkable contraption which takes boats down to the River Weaver in huge caissons.

Leaving Digles Basin on the Worcester and Birmingham Canal to join the River Severn. Inland waterways are an irresistible attraction to children and a boatload will provide plenty of willing hands for mooring and locking.

Warwick, a modern steel narrow boat built on traditional lines, travels a lonely stretch of the Macclesfield Canal, near Bosley.

Leaving a lock on the Macclesfield Canal.

On the Kennet and Avon Canal at Newbury. This once formed a through route from the Thames at Reading to the Bristol Channel via the River Avon at Bath. Unfortunately, much of the waterway was allowed to become derelict, but strenuous efforts are now being made to re-open it from end to end. In the meantime, it is navigable only in isolated sections.

Canals come in all shapes and sizes—some are officially described as 'wide' waterways, a classification applied more to the width of the locks than the actual channel. Some 'wide' canals have only a narrow navigable trench in the middle and silted banks. Conversely, some 'narrow' canals have wide sections. The Ashby Canal is narrow and shallow throughout and, at times, also weedy but this is part of its attraction. Although originally built to carry coal from collieries at Ashby-de-la-Zouch, it winds through completely rural surroundings.

St CANUTE
FOWEY

On the Regents Canal at Paddington Basin, in the heart of London, two converted narrow boats carry visitors on trips along the city's canal system.

·own in the West Country is the Exeter Canal, probably the oldest man-made water- ·ay in the country. In the early fourteenth century a weir was built across the river xe, by Isabella, Countess of Devon, blocking navigation to the sea. Consequently, ıe Corporation of Exeter obtained an Act for a canal to bypass the weir and this was ompleted in 1566. This picture shows the massive lift bridge recently built, ·hich carries the A38 traffic.

:entred on the canal basin below the town is the Exeter Maritime Museum, full of ıscinating exhibits from all over the world. Many types of craft—inland and seagoing -are preserved and exhibited in ideal surroundings. These range from the fine old team tug in the picture, to a pearling dhow and reed boat from Lake Titicaca.

A small boat in a large lock, at Stoke Bruerne on the Grand Union Canal in Northamptonshire. One of the buildings in the background houses the Waterways Museum, a fascinating collection of items dating back to the heyday of the canal era. The museum was opened in 1963 and is visited by thousands of people every year—both by road and canal. Undoubtedly one of the most interesting exhibits is a full scale section of a narrow boat *Sunny Valley*, with the tiny cabin furnished as it would have been when lived in.

Elton, a working narrow boat, moored alongside the Waterways Museum, having carried a load of cement for minor building repairs. The other buildings in the area form an interesting collection, ranging from a fine old waterside pub, 'The Boat', to warehouses and a shop.

The Caledonian Canal runs straight across Scotland from north-east to south-west through the Great Glen. It was designed to provide a short, safe route from the North Sea to the Atlantic, avoiding the hazardous Pentland Firth.

The canal route was surveyed by Thomas Telford in 1801 and work commenced three years later on the 22 miles of man-made section. The remaining 38 miles consists of natural lochs—Lochs Ness, Oich and Lochy. The complete canal from Inverness to Fort William was opened

A cruiser crossing the wide expanse of Loch Ness with the sun shining on Fort Augustus and snow-capped hills in the background.

in 1822 and was a major engineering feat of its day.

Nowadays, it is used by the occasional cargo boat and quite a number of fishing vessels which often cover the whole length in one day. It is becoming increasingly popular for pleasure cruising and although it is probably not suitable for the complete novice (there are a few navigational difficulties), anyone with even limited experience could spend a wonderful holiday on this magnificent waterway.

A quiet mooring below Invergarry Castle on Loch Oich.

There is a staircase of five massive locks at Fort Augustus, capable of taking half a dozen fishing boats at a time. Fortunately, all locks and swing bridges are manned and it is a fascinating sight from a boat to see the massive road and rail bridges swung aside, apparently effortlessly, to allow free passage.

A 'Project 31' cruiser of the Caley Cruiser hire fleet, based at Inverness, here moored in the canal close to the entrance of Loch Lochy. These are sea-going craft fully equipped with navigational aids, including echo sounders, compasses, etc.

LAKES AND RIVERS

Every stretch of navigable water in Britain probably supports a few boats of one sort or another and everyone will have his, or her, favourite lake or river. It is impossible to mention here more than a few of the more popular areas.

Some rivers—the Wye, for example—are suitable only for canoes, others, such as the Severn, can be used by large commercial craft and the locks are built on a suitably massive scale.

Windermere Lake, below, is ten miles from end to end and is set amidst magnificent scenery. Craft can be hired, or launched at various points around the lake. It is worth remembering that extensive areas of inland water can become surprisingly rough in high winds and that one does not have the room to manœuvre that exists at sea, or in estuaries. Although there are no worries about tides, moorings and anchorages need to be chosen with an eye to any possible change in wind direction, or strength, overnight.

Shakespeare's Avon is a pleasant river. Slow-flowing between low banks, it allows views across meadows to small villages and distant hills. The towns that do encroach along its banks are friendly places with an unhurried atmosphere.

The river is entered through Avon Lock at Tewkesbury, by turning out of the River Severn past Healing's Mill (watch for shallows on the bend). Once through the lock, which is manned, there are pleasant moorings on the town side of King John's Bridge, ideal for visiting this fascinating old town with its half-timbered houses and ancient abbey.

The boats in the picture above are leaving Avon Lock and swinging out into the short section leading to the Severn.

In 1950, the Lower Avon Navigation Trust took over responsibility for navigation between Tewkesbury and Evesham. Many of the locks were derelict and these have gradually been rebuilt over the years with the assistance of voluntary labour. Similarly, magnificent work has been carried out by the Upper Avon Navigation Trust on the stretch between Evesham and Stratford and in June 1974 their efforts were rewarded when the whole navigation was re-opened, thus providing a superb cruising circular route taking in the rivers Avon and Severn, and associated canals. Stratford-upon-Avon is now once again linked with the sea. There is a good restaurant with moorings in peaceful surroundings alongside Fladbury Bridge.

Angling is popular everywhere on the Avon, but perhaps nowhere more than on the stretch of bank adjoining the old bridge at Pershore.

The River Severn is wide and deep, with high banks in many places which, unfortunately, tend to restrict the view from the river. Nevertheless, it is a waterway well worth cruising with interesting towns conveniently spaced along its banks. Worcester is dominated by the tower of its ancient cathedral, as in the picture above looking downstream. The entrance to the Worcester and Birmingham Canal (mentioned earlier) is just around the bend on the left, through a lock gate that appears small against the massive structures on the Severn. Digles Severn Locks—two in parallel—are about half a mile farther down the river.

Worcester is a busy city and traffic moves continuously through its crowded streets and over the main road bridge. After an expedition to the shops it is pleasant to return to the quiet of one's own boat moored well away from the noise and commotion. There are good public moorings about a quarter of a mile above the road bridge, a hundred yards or so above a rail bridge.

Lastly, a river that is a canal—or perhaps a canal that is really a river! The River Wey is navigable from Godalming to its junction with the Thames at Shepperton. Its route follows partly the natural course of the river and there are also man-made sections of canal, with numerous locks. One of the two waterways owned by the National Trust (the other is the Stratford-upon-Avon Canal), it passes through delightful rural countryside, although running quite close to several large towns. Here a boat passes through a typical lock late in the year, with a row of moored craft extending into the distance, most no doubt already laid up for the winter.